Half the Hurricanes

Praise for Half the Hurricanes

"Evie Groch is a poet, a teacher, a traveler, and a feminist. In her new collection of poetry, her well-crafted poems are strong, powerful hurricanes that spin around us, pulling us into her world. In the first poem, *Rooted in Defiance*, Evie writes, *I have mastered every survival skill, and my mantra has become: Rebel and refuse to grow in rows.* I like her attitude! Read this book and enjoy the storm."

>JOHANNA ELY
>
>Poet Laureate Emerita of Benicia, California

"As 'summer exhales in tiny hisses' so does this book of poems. This is a collection that will teach you how to 'listen to the language of the trees.' The journeys inside this book remind us how vital are the footholds of our ancestry, language, food and culture. As you travel the stanzas, you will encounter Mendocino farms, yeast that never rose, Iowa plains, and the indelible the sound of crickets. As you turn each page, you will find a necessary escape to international panties, burros on the roadside, and a highway paved in hope. You will hear music inside this collection as if 'from a distant land, the pull of ancient silk threads.'"

>CONNIE POST
>
>Author of *Floodwater*, winner of the Lyrebird Award, and *Prime Meridian*, finalist in the International Book Awards
>
>Poet Laureate Emerita of Livermore, California

Half the Hurricanes

POEMS

Evie Groch

© 2022 by Evie Groch

All rights reserved. No part of this publication may be reproduced, stored in a retrieval system, or transmitted in any form or by any means, electronic, mechanical, photocopying, recording, or otherwise, without the prior written permission of the publisher.

ISBN 978-1-939030-10-8

Cover art by Chris Read

Oakledge Press
Hercules, California
www.oakledge-press.com

To Carl
for his solid support
and delightful distractions

Contents

Rooted in Defiance 1

Imperatives 2

Mămăligă 3

On the Road to Marrakesh 4

Infusion 6

Communication in a Foreign Language Class 8

Good News 10

Villanelle for a Coffee Queen 12

Wicked Music 13

Mr. Rogers Doesn't Live Here 14

Over Dinner 16

Heat, Not Warmth 18

Filtering 19

The Greatest Benefit to Humankind 20

My International Pantry 22

A Coat of Many Collars 24

Bábushka 26

The Invisible Synagogue in Lima 27

No Humor in Poems 28

A Recipe for Rotwelsch 30

In the Cupboard 32

What I Found Under the Bridge 34

Estranged Sisters	35
The Array	36
Uncertain Prayer	38
Six Feet of Perpetual Motion	40
Borkis	42
Journey of Souls	44
The Longest Thirty-Mile Drive	46
The Gathering Gene	48
Reversal of Misfortune	49
Stems	50
The Son He Never Had	52
Nature's Embrace	54
The Message in the Movement	55
Barrett Avenue Bus Stop	56
Summary of Senses	58
Fading	59
Beat	60
Truth or Dare	62
Droplet	64
Kintsukuroi	65
Leaves on a Stone Fence	66
Pride without the Fall	67
Bless Me	68

Spare Me	70
A City in the Stans of Central Asia	71
Evidence of the Wind	72
Charcoal and Chalk	73
Economy of Words	74
F is for Fiction	75
The Other Parent	76
Trespassers All	78
Gladiolas in a White Vase	79
Bursting with Pride	80
Curtains	81
Left Hanging in a Web	82
2020 Hindsight	84
Mendocino Farms Sandwich Market	86
Vellichor	88
No Rhyme nor Reason	89
My Tsunami	90
Sounds of August	92
A Tablespoon of Salt	93
Postcards and Bananas	94
Summer at a Price	95
Half the Hurricanes	96
Lessons from an Uneducated Master	98

Fading From View 100
When Notes Become a Melody 101
Arrival 102
Acknowledgments 105
About the Author 107

Preface

What I cannot express in prose, I divulge in poems. They measure my pulse, give hues to my moods, share my fears, reflect my values, amuse, and evidence my change. Bringing them together, a daunting challenge, I find they make me bigger than the sum of their stanzas and offer me a drop of immortality.

Rooted in Defiance

I have survived drought, neglect,
drenching, and hatred.
No one wants me near them,
not on their property,
not on their golf courses.

Most find me undesirable,
in the wrong place,
unwelcome, aggressive.

The only thing I'm envied for
is my easy adaptation
to habitats harsh and severe.
I dare to go places others shun
and thrive in disturbance.
I resist eradication and survive
to compete and outlast.

I have mastered every survival skill,
and my mantra has become:
Rebel and refuse to grow in rows.
Plant your salacious self in yesterday's
garden of weeds and become one yourself.

Published in *Quintessence*, Soul Poet Society, June 2021

Imperatives

Come, step into the light with me,
hear the breeze carry the seagull's
wing's swoop.
Linger with me in sunshine pouring
generously over hills,
painting golden the curves of the land.
Look with me at weeds praying
to become grass,
searching for the green that water brings.
Wait with me until dark
unveils the stars,
features them as sequins in a navy cape.
Inhale with me the spray
of sea on the coast,
the saline smell of waves
coming ashore.
Grasp my hand as I lead you
into the calm of the woods
to listen to the language of trees.
Do this and I'll never ask
another thing of you.

Judge's Favorite, Alameda County Fair, 2021

Published in *Whimsical Poet: A Journal of Contemporary Poetry*, June 1, 2021

MĂMĂLIGA

Mama fed me porridge
made of yellow maize flour, *mămăliga*,
peasant food from eastern Europe
to stave off hunger.
In the States, she never made it.
It gave away our status.

Fine dining became our pastime,
we ate out quite often,
a dish called polenta in high demand.
I savored it, found out why.
My *mămăliga* was back in vogue,
with a gourmet's touch.

Refusing to eat it herself, my mother
smiled every time she heard me order it.

Published in *Sage Soup*, Issue 1, 2021

On the Road to Marrakesh

A highway paved in hope,
a destination of promise.
Cemeteries litter the roadside
in a manner disrespectful
to the departed.
National police in sharp gray
uniforms trimmed in red
with pilot hats stop
traffic to flex muscle.
Sheep and their goat cousins
sample breakfast
under stoic, farsighted
eyes of herders.
Burros on the roadside
eternally, mindlessly pulling
carts of produce, wares.
Overloaded transport trucks
list, drip ropes which trail them
in their wake.
Honks announcing passing
on the musical staff of lanes,
vagrants disguised as
highway workers reap litter
from the median like crops –
a day's work till the evening
break from the fast of Ramadan.
Dry lands like preheated ovens
coat tiers with sagebrush brown.

Anticipation grows
water for parched throats,
shade for weary souls,
couscous in the tagine for dinner.
How soon, Marrakesh.

Published in *The High Window*, Winter 2021

Infusion

It came alive in hot water.
Tea would sit still, outwait him.
He didn't like it strong,
never used a pot.
He placed the bag in a clear
glass, stirred with a metal
spoon 'til the liquid tanned to the
desired color. The spoon stayed.
A single cube of sugar tucked in his cheek
sweetened the beverage
sipped through that side of his mouth.
Just like in the old country.
Over and over I watched him,
a man with a custom he learned
from his papa and older brother.

I shared his beverage when I was ill,
or weak, or needed healing.
I broke with custom when
I left home, went to college,
guzzled coffee with abandon, caffeine
my steady friend on eve of finals.

He comes to mind each time
I'm offered a choice of one or the other
and pick the one he would not drink.
A disloyal daughter? Or one who
was lured to robust aromas
by her husband, who now
has taken up tea.

Tasters waver, go back and forth,
but I remain devout just like
my father who was nothing
if not steeped in tradition.

Published in *Life and Legends,* 10th edition, June 15, 2021

Communication in a Foreign Language Class

The most disengaged student
in my classroom
had no words to share with me.

His glazed-over eyes told me Spanish
had no value. Science was his language.
His mother tongue, English.
His heritage, Chinese.
His ability level, genius,
acing every test,
but mute to conversation,
the backbone of the course.

The doodling in his margins
caught my eye in passing.
A Star Trek communicator?
Could it really be?

You're a Trekkie, I blurted out.
His eyes popped open wide.
That was all it took.
Like Sulu on the Enterprise,
we switched to code of starships.

Each day he'd show up early,
homemade communicator in hand
emitting a familiar sound.
Another day a phaser, deliberately set on stun.
After school a script he wrote
for Paramount he hoped.

We found our common language,
then he dialogued in Castilian,
taught me a lesson I needed to learn.
Once I embraced his passion
he unmuted himself to me.

Good News

Every Sunday, a one-hour visit,
one hour to watch her wrestle with truth,
one hour to convince her she is wrong,
to listen to her fears, fail again to reassure.

Where are my parents, she asks,
she, a woman in her eighties.
Will they be here soon?
I need to get dressed; help me please.
What time are they coming?
I'll need to leave.

Mom, your parents won't be coming.
They're not around anymore.
This is where you live now.
I come to visit you every Sunday.

I watch her heart sink with the news,
it does so every week.
Devastation, shock, denial, sadness,
offers of *But I'm here* don't help.

Next Sunday I return to hear
Where are my parents?
Will they be here soon?
I need to get dressed; help me please
What time are they coming?
I'll need to leave.

Weary of fighting, I say
They'll be here soon.
You look nice in what you're wearing.
Shall we have some tea
in the dining hall while we wait?

A warm glow bathes her face,
she smiles and looks at me anew,
touches my face as angst leaves hers
and tea flows down her parched throat
while tears flow down my cheeks.

First Place Award, Marin County Fair, 2019

Villanelle for a Coffee Queen

On alcohol I am not keen
I am not even tempted
I have a broken drinking gene

There, now at last I have come clean
I crave not scotch, want no vodka
On alcohol I am not keen

My whiskey-bringing friends I screen
They all can drink their fill at home
I have a broken drinking gene

So much hard liquor I have seen
At my wedding so long ago
On alcohol I am not keen

Still unopened, sealed and obscene
Bottles stand in our cabinet
I have a broken drinking gene

But you could tempt me with caffeine
I'm not a total Philistine
On alcohol I am not keen
I have a broken drinking gene

Wicked Music

A deliberate winter wind from the dark side
of distant moons blows down to earth,
travels through ozone holes, from mountain
tops to gorges deep, across the Steppe,
Gobi Desert, Iowa plains, tundra, glaciers,
lands down under, through abandoned mines,
under rocks, and into ravines.
Scoops up idle gossip, quips from icy lips,
malevolent auras, ill intent, whines,
whispers, groans, curses and prayers of doom.

Lands them in the evening trees
where they dangle from shaking branches
like an unbalanced mobile.

If you listen sleeplessly, you can hear
it play sour notes on an atonal keyboard.

Published by *The Wild Word* in its Winter Song issue,
December 2020

Mr. Rogers Doesn't Live Here

House hunting, my agent asks
What are you looking for?
Which neighborhood is calling you?
Which style do you adore?

My ideal, I share with her
comes from a list I made.
Although it's well thought out,
it's picky I'm afraid.

Next door would live the journalist
forever checking facts.
Two doors down, an essayist,
enjoys his own wisecracks.

On the corner, a novelist
who spins full tales of fiction.
Eight doors down, a poetess
with powers of depiction.

Backing up to my own house,
an editor of note
who polices words and voice,
an error can make him gloat.

Four doors up, a columnist
who gets paid by the inch.
At times his themes elude him –
he finds himself in a pinch.

A short story writer
is somewhere in between,
and I, the memoirist,
would simply serve as queen.

This is where I choose to live
and welcome all who knock,
for then I shall not ever fear
having a writers' block.

3rd Place Award, Ina Coolbrith Memorial Poetry Prize, 2014

Over Dinner

Words used to overflow in our simmering dialogues
and continue on a low rolling boil until they exhausted
themselves and dribbled down our lips and chin
to land in our lap on a napkin we would fold up
and carry away with us to ensure some leftover
sparing for later in the evening.

The silence of the seasoned pairs around us
made us wonder what happened to their words.

Of late we start the meal with pleasantries –
Your day? The food? Any calls?
We scan the radar screens for blips we can respond to.
I share how I was made to feel by a friend I'll no longer keep
or repeat a clever comeback I heard on an outing,
looking for validation and attention.

He unpacks his political bag, and out tumble
the idiotic quotes from inane candidates
ready to transport us back a century or two.
He provides the strop for honing my sarcasm,
and I find enough vinegar and acid within me
to marinate my barbs before skewering the tripe
before me and removing it from the table.

Our new nightly ritual – after he loads up on TV's
angry-men quips, we grind them into our salt shakers
and sprinkle them on our portions to wake up our buds
and season our thoughts.

What will we do if peace ever breaks out?
The dinner dialogue will suffer,
but we'll practice our well-honed flirting rituals
in the comfort we've built over fifty years of love.

Honorable Mention, Alameda County Fair, 2016

HEAT, NOT WARMTH

Sun-seared sidewalks
pray for shelter
under sheets of rust-colored dust.
Sandal-clad feet
bronzed by a Moroccan furnace
make their stamp
on unpaved paths.
A sip of water
is a sin,
a glance too long – a dare.
We're not clad
as modest women,
and so deserve the stares
and taunts.
Men mouth *welcome*,
but their eyes say otherwise.
They practice patience
as they sit and wait for sundown.
Ramadan in Casablanca.

Filtering

My brain is on, the tap is open, clear water is coming as we wait for the passing.
Rust
Drivel
Silt
Clichés
Rust
Babble
Dirt
Dust
Rust
The tap is open, my brain is on, clear water is coming as we wait for the passing.

Published by *The Skinny Poetry Journal,* June 2016

The Greatest Benefit to Humankind

Girls doing science are like bears riding bikes.
Possible, but freakish.
(from a graduate school advisor to his female student
in *The Overstory*)

To humankind's benefit, the nobelists Ghez, Charpentier,
and Doudna turned a deaf ear on this comparison,
putting it swiftly to shame.
Not relegated to simply nibbling on the Milky Way,
horoscoping, clearing dust as a domestic,
getting her hair waved at certain lengths,
Ghez pioneered a path in Physics, was just
awarded a shared Nobel Prize for her discovery
of a black hole in our galaxy. They call it Sagittarius A.

She imaged infrared wavelengths,
visible light once blocked by heavy dust,
now seen by her.
An advisor has been schooled.

Once considered girls who play
with building blocks,
soft science literary pundits,
seamstresses with shears
on which to practice,
Charpentier and Doudna
split the Nobel Prize in Chemistry
to correct disease-causing mutations,
applicable to building blocks of life.
Their discovery of clustered regularly
interspaced short palindromic repeats
(Crispr) offers genetic scissors to snip
out damaged DNA molecules.

Reverberating messages to young girls:
Help rid the circus of bicycle riding bears,
and teach the naysayers that the word
freakish now describes them.

Published in *They Call Us: Feminine Literary Magazine*, Edition #3, Winter 2021.

My International Pantry

Hungarian paprika stands tall and proud,
Makes my chicken *ez finom,* no blandness allowed.

French onion soup is *de rigueur,*
Flavors my roast in no manner obscure.

Israeli couscous has pearl appeal,
Screams *mazel tov* in a good mouth feel.

German chocolate cake mix on the shelf,
Yells a loud *achtung* – help yourself.

Kikkoman panko leaves a trail of crumbs,
Says *sayonara* to its shelf mate chums.

In the back I find my Indian curry,
so needed for my *svādiṣṭa* chicken tandoori.

My Pompeian extra virgin olive oil
says *ciao* to its roots in Italian soil.

Irish whiskey – a drop in our *daingean* coffee
pairs well with the sweetness of elastic toffee.

Truly American and getting top billing
is our all-time favorite – apple pie filling.

When I plan a meal I have my passport handy
to travel through the pantry like a child choosing candy.

I enter simply to fill my pot,
but I come out a polyglot.

3rd Place Award, Ina Coolbrith Memorial Poetry Prize, 2015

A Coat of Many Collars

Pathways of pain spin
with strands of fear,
weave together, create
a mantel I wear upon my shoulders
with a stiff upturned collar
more priestly than canine
that reflects the ages of angst
and stages of doubt
that etched their traces
into my face and mind,
sank deep my eyes,
stooped my posture –
this mantel, an artifact
of a life endured,
accepted with spoonfuls
of equilibrium and resignation.

The time is right
for a wardrobe change,
for a cape soaked in salve,
a collar soft and smooth,
that cradles, comforts,
lies gently on the slopes.
A cape threaded with intermittent
joys peeking through seams,
worn as a healing cloth
to smooth over the jagged edges
of a profile shattered in free fall
and pieced together with intention.

2nd Place, Division 360—Poetry Contest, Class 2,
San Mateo County Fair, 2018

BÁBUSHKA

Over and over they refer to me that way.
It carries a sweetness that isn't old-lady-like,
endearing and respectful
allowing for a display of spunk.
My age is forever in question
for strangers and new acquaintances alike –
blunt requests from men and women.
When I hesitate, they're lost.
Why they ask in innocence.
In America you never ask a woman her age
I hear myself explain to the deaf,
then I realize we're not in America
but in Uzbekistan
and perhaps I am the one who isn't listening.
I give my age.

First Place, Marin County Fair, 2017

The Invisible Synagogue in Lima

Guido walks the three of us
from our hotel on Sunday
to take in the small synagogue
sitting in a sleepy setting.
You can't miss it, they all said,
but had he not walked us,
we would have missed it.
A pale blue one-story building
encased in a steel-rodded outer gate,
windows covered.
It sits silently in the calm of a cool morning,
devoid of symbols, markings, name plate,
signs of welcome.
Locked, shuttered, cloaked in anonymity.
Our gut fills in the story,
and we are saddened to understand
the need to hide as in centuries past.

No Humor in Poems

I've been cautioned,
Write no poems of humor.
Avoid irony, sarcasm, puns
or cleverness; they'll
never earn you kudos,
will irritate the elite poets.

I ask myself
Why write at all
if what I love is banned?
Better to ask a bird to limit its takeoffs,
a bovine to enjoy a cudless chew,
a bee to visit pollen-free flowers,
tigers and zebras to erase their stripes.

Tell me where I don't belong,
and that's the door I'll knock on.
Tell me what not to do,
and I will get it done.
Belittle me, and I'll make you
the vortex of my verse,
the villain of my villanelle,
the fiend in my iambic feet.

I kid you not, but if I did
you'd take this all in jest,
perhaps catch yourself stifling
a smile, a private giggle,
or a smirk you hide in public.

We've earned our stripes,
cannot be stripped of them,
the tigers, zebras, birds, bovines,
bees and I. It's what we do.
It's who we are.

A Recipe for Rotwelsch

On the road eternally
escaping to nowhere,
relying on *zinken** for sustenance,
a sign to welcome the stranger,
the peddler, tinker, grinder,
those with no abode,
itinerant speakers who applied
the lesson of Babel to birth
a recipe for an almost language–
a sociolect.
Equal parts Yiddish, Hebrew,
repurposed German,
a concoction cooked up to speak
openly in code and safety,
a linguistic mixing enraging elites,
keeping outsiders in the dark,
binding community members
together in unique speech.

This is Rotwelsch, the incomprehensible
language of beggars,
language with no grammar,
no literature, nothing in writing,
designed to evade capture by scholars,
a language predicated on estrangement,
on moving meaning,
a punch in the face to German,
Martin Luther, and centuries of persecution.
Like an obsession, it draws me in
for reasons I cannot express.

* from the Latin *signum* for sign, pictograms carved into fence posts or chalked on houses (a cross inside a circle), signifying the occupants would feed you.

Published in *Life and Legends,* 10th edition, June 15, 2021

In the Cupboard

On the table among the New Gamboge,
Winsor Lemon, and Permanent Rose
lie brushes pointed and rounded
near water cups of Prussian Blue
and Jasper Green.

We paint with broad strokes
and detailed attention
the broccoli heads and tangelos
slinking across the models' table.

We remember to color wash
and define by negative space,
we focus on the table
and suffer no distractions.

Until the teacher opens the cupboard
to reach the empty yogurt containers
and I espy a pair of red and white stilettos –
stilettos with 4-inch heels, which rest perpendicularly
on the shelf and whisper for someone to set them free,
take them out and dance hard.

I cannot shift my eyes.
Broccoli can wait.
Who left the shoes?
In a cupboard of discards which
patiently wait their turn to prance and spin,
they plead for mercy and move me like no
tangelo can.

First Place, Free Verse, San Mateo County Fair, 2013

What I Found Under the Bridge

A world of shadows, darkness of souls,
life in crude details, implausible depths,
tears of regret, sinking dreams,
atonal symphonies of the night,
cloaks of doom,
a crumbling ceiling of despair,
a black canvas awaiting a drop of sun,
marinating puddles of sorrow,
trolls awaiting their fee and my tumble –
everything but water.

Honorable Mention, Division 360—Poetry Contest, Class 2,
San Mateo County Fair, 2016

Estranged Sisters

So in tune with one another
they exist only twelve strikes apart
twins separated at birth
sporting identical hues
violets and blues
dripping orange, streaking red
framed by softly lit grays
on a canvas of washed colors
yet they've never met
these siblings named Dawn and Dusk.

The Array

I approach Starbucks for my meeting,
the crowd unusually large.
What is this on an average Tuesday?
Who the heck's in charge?

I hear the whispers as I draw near.
Folks are talking sexy.
He's not wearing much, they say,
But causing some apoplexy.

I wait my turn, sneak a peek,
try to glance up front.
The line is thick, can't see a thing,
"Wait your turn!" they're blunt.

Finally he comes into view
inside the glass pastry display
wearing nothing but a Speedo,
and living a cliché.

He's young, buff, and totally ripped;
He strikes a pose and flexes.
All the women take a breath
yet this affects both sexes.

I stare at him inside the counter
among the sweet array:
bran, pumpkin, banana cupcakes
wonder what he would weigh.

Among the muffins, I see English,
vegan and lemon poppy seed,
blueberry, cranberry orange,
more than anyone could need.

I buy my mocha, leave the store
making my way through the crowd.
When others ask why the line
I say, "Wait, you'll be wowed."

"So many pastries for you to choose,
but there's one you will adore,
just be patient and don't push."
"Wait" they say, "tell us more."

"Choose your muffin carefully;
one may land with a thud,
and that would be a special one,
a muffin they call Stud."

Uncertain Prayer

Fearful that nature will not survive us,
I am lured to the undulating floor
of a cathedral of trees,
the russet canopy a colander straining
sun rays, allowing light to drip through
and announce the morning in earnest.

One sapling bullies its way into belonging;
others observe with patience, no judgment.
Nursing logs, the altars for rituals,
offer comfort and sustenance
to congregants unsure of prayer.
They gather by need, by awe, by chance,
stunned by rainbow streaks of lichen
spattered on these maternal platforms
from a divine bucket of paint.

No choir, no organ – trees tune the winter wind,
create a symphony of motion,
movements with no baton,
orchestrated by grass roots.

I focus on the intricate lace connecting
trees in the morning brilliance,
the dewy vision a web
woven by a vacant landlord.

Leaving the forest, I see a sky
so thick with blue it seems
smeared on with finger paints.
My fears allayed, my hope restored,
I linger on the path that takes
the long way home.

Published in *Quintessence*, Soul Poet Society, June 2021

Published by *The Wild Word* in its Winter Song issue, December 2020

Six Feet of Perpetual Motion

He's never fazed by rain or sleet
Programmed to deliver
No giving up
Not in his plan
He hurries on the path
With cargo to unload

He may get a tan
Or turn bright red
As he legs along his route
Strong anchoring skills
Lifting above his weight
Marches alone or with peers
To carry out his duty

Prepositions of choice
Guide his way –
If not through, then around
Above or below
A blocked path
No deterrent
A detour will suffice
You can't deter him
Can't break his will
Home is the hill
He'll die on

Slippage of rubble
Needs just a sidestep
A social creature in his heart
Out for picnics or on hikes
Not a welcome site to others
On blankets or in their home
A total spoiler he can be
Above all in your p-ANT-ry.

BORKIS

My *mameh* called them *borkis*,
bought them by the pound at Von's,
the supermarket in the ghetto,
toted them home in her two-wheeled
folding shopping cart.
The deeper the red,
the darker the burgundy,
the richer the taste,
or so she would have me believe.

As she ribboned off their skins,
she inhaled their scent,
prided herself in their smooth nakedness,
prepared them for their bath.

Dry the *borkis*, mash them, add the juice,
season them, serve them cold
with a side of mashed potatoes.
Other cooks in the ghetto did the same,
a similar aroma wafting from house to house
marking them as "others."

Forced to sip this "specialty" she prepared for him,
I struggled to swallow, watching my dad
enjoy his borscht as I could only picture
peasants 'round the hearth. A shameful taste,
a stigma tattooed on my tongue, indelible,
bloody red with shame.

I still avoid them today
at Raley's produce section,
no longer in the ghetto,
but willing to skip a beet.

Selected for publication in *Sage Soup*, Issue 1, 2021

Journey of Souls

Our boat mutely moves toward
ritual funereal pyres
along the shores of the Ganges
where cremations flame with brightness.
They celebrate in Varanasi
like nowhere else: chanting, drumbeats,
wails, prayers at the water's edge.

White-robed priests under lit arches
sway in unison to mystical rhythms.
Shoreline alive with color and form.

Ambience hyper normal, slightly magical.
Low billows of gray smoke
puff out from newly extinguished burns
next to raging hot bonfires.

Corpses lined up for their final sendoff,
first by fire, then by water
as they slide into the Ganges.

Profiles of bereaved families
in shadows glow softly in their candlelight
as ceremonies fade into memories.

We hold a candlelit flower petal,
each of us setting one to sail.
Soon they are specks of light,
stars in a dark aspic of salinity.

Published in *Life and Legends*, 10th edition, June 15, 2021

The Longest Thirty-Mile Drive

A mid-morning phone call interrupts my writing.
A sincere sounding social worker mispronounces
our surname as she verifies I am Carl's wife
and steadies herself to deliver in the fewest
number of words news I do not want to hear.
Your husband was in an accident.
This is the third time I have received a message like this.
The Orbea bicycle has betrayed him again.

I steel myself before I break the silence on her end,
hoping she won't continue with an additional sentence
that might collapse my world.
Is   he   alive? I whisper.
Yes, he is.
Is   he   conscious?
I do not know.
I'm on my way.

The number of minutes from the phone call
from John Muir Hospital to my arrival in the trauma center
is no less than a lifetime.
I make a conscious effort not to speed,
for how will that improve the outcome?
Traffic is at its slowest,
no one cares how quickly I need to arrive.
The minute hand on my wrist seems to have stalled,
and red taillights outline my path.

I swipe left on scenarios that pop up in my brain,
wishing I could click on "delete all,"
but the loop continues until I pull into Emergency
only to be told to go park in the structure.
I meekly obey because I need the time
to compose and dry my eyes.

I go through a thorough check: hand sanitizing,
temperature taking, ID checking, until his ER
bed number is divulged like a spy's code word
and a visitor sticker is stuck to my chest.
I make my way up the elevator,
two occupants at a time standing diagonally apart
and exit onto his floor.
The French hospital doors are locked,
and I must pick up the phone to ask for admittance.
Who are you and whom do you want to see?
As I approach his bed, I inhale and ask for strength.
A nurse is at my side, preparing me to greet
my husband of 53 years. I have only minutes
before I have to step out again so an epidural
can be inserted for a morphine drip.

I step in resolutely, determined not to show
a trace of weakness or worry.
He sees me, he's conscious, thank God!
He is in a royal collar, his neck immobilized
as he mouths the words to me, *I'm sorry.*

Honorable Mention, San Mateo County Fair, 2021

The Gathering Gene

Now that normal has been evicted
it's up to us foraging sisters
to step out into the fear to gather food,
sustain the clan,
restore humanity and humility,
unite the citizenry, dispel the lies.

We speak softly with thoughtful words,
tread lightly against threats,
lure insults back from the brink,
plan a path toward a pandemic of trust.
We know what others still must learn:
Fires, tornadoes, tsunamis
cannot be bullied into submission.
Neither can viruses.

So let us put on our hardship boots,
lift our shields,
march out with compassion
and an outstretched arm
to show what caring, intelligent
leaders can do.
Lace 'em up, ladies.

Published in *In the Midst: A Covid-19 Anthology,* Inspiration for Writers, Inc., November 2020

Reversal of Misfortune

Run me backwards to catch my drift
Read me from right to left
I precede myself in time and space
Am not on standard dials

I am the thunder before the lightning
The bite before the bark
The crashing tree before the axe
The scream before the pain

I am the flying golf ball before the *fore!*
The bleeding before the cut
The burial before the slaughter
The echo before the sound

I am shell-shock before the combat
The scar before the surgery
The indigestion before the meal
The effect before the cause

I am the prayer for forgiveness before the sin
The damage before the warning
The nightmare before the Holocaust
By the time you hear me, it's already too late.

Published in *The Pangolin Review,* Issue 3.5, 2018

Accepted for publication in *Balm 2, Psythur,* Ravens Quoth Press

Stems

I come from polyglots
who drew the line at English.
I learned the words
they hid from me
in tongues exotic, complex.
I crossed the line they drew.

In me they planted a seed
of caution when treading
on unfriendly shores,
and all shores were unfriendly.
Choose carefully the tongue
you wag in public.
Don't call attention to yourself
with evil tongue, "lashon hara."
Stay close to home,
don't go looking for enemies,
they're right next door.

I wasted decades on inattention
to their oppressors and those they
were forced to leave behind.
Pogroms drove many out, bigots
identified the rest, nazis stepped
in to finish them off.
And now there are few to find
in this continent foreign to me,
still threatening as it was for them.

My parents' oppressors have
come ashore in my new home,
and I need to call them out,
expose them for what they are
and used to be.

First Place Award for earlier version, San Mateo Country Fair, 2018

The Son He Never Had

With a wink and a grin he always said
You're like the son I never had.
I basked in those words,
so proud my father elevated me
to a status so high,
a status most daughters couldn't reach.

I earned that praise – accompanied
him to work sites, helped him
clean vacated apartments,
went on walks with him
to visit his friends on the corner.

I even wielded a hammer,
sanded wood, painted walls,
learned to drive the Chevy
at fourteen under his keen eye,
a secret just between the two of us.

He conveyed to me there was
nothing I couldn't do.
and I believed him.
And then, after becoming
a mother of two girls,
I started to wonder.

Why hadn't he appreciated me
for the daughter I was?
It was too late to ask,
but he could have said,
You're the daughter I always wanted,
and that would have sufficed.

Published in *Writing in a Woman's Voice,* October 10, 2020

Nature's Embrace

In a fold in the hills lies
my home, tugged awake
at dawn by slender
twists of fog.
They slip through my blinds
and massage my view.
I face the day
through a filter
of gentle anticipation
as my horizon widens
and my focus sharpens.
In time I came to accept
the ways of the hills
and to allow the fog
to tuck me in its blanket
for the night.

The Message in the Movement

A dance is a dance
but flamenco is spirit in flame,
arched spine of strength
spreads shivers to stomping feet,
fingers caress castanets,
pulse out codes that hypnotize
with staccato rhythms
yet preserve a delicate beckoning
to engage in a rendezvous.
Petticoats of white foam
accent the elusive hem of a
dress sewn to entice the romance
out of the underground and into which
a body is poured ounce by ounce
to move to the wails and claps
of the *canteflamenco*.
A *pericón* behind which to hide her face,
a *peineta* to crown her head,
an unchained force that claims the stage.
A dance is a dance
but flamenco is raw, unrobed romance.

Selected for publication by *Open Door Magazine,* March 6, 2021

BARRETT AVENUE BUS STOP

Sometimes talking breaks out. I watch them
from my window as they await the public wheels.
Just above the tennis courts, one and one-half blocks
below the snaking route Arlington Boulevard provides
traversing the hills from Richmond to Berkeley,
early travelers of the casteless society gather to wait.
The nanny with her charge keeps her distance
from a backpacked student munching Doritos
unwittingly feeding the scavengers with his droppings.
The man in his three-piece suit
must be interviewing in the city again.
The cook in the stately house, in her penguin walk,
armed with recycled bags, heads for the organic
farmer's market.
Preteen girls share Droid earbuds, united
by their love of Bruno Mars.
The young athlete bounces a basketball
the driver will ask him to hold onto.
A visitor tries to find himself on his unfolded map.

In the early evening the cleaning lady appears
with her canvas briefcase of tools.
A bespectacled gentleman whose beret and corduroy jacket
lend him a casual professorial look, with his nose
buried in a dog-eared book
does his best to ignore a tatted millennial
with nose ring and spiked blue hair beside him.

A couple looks at their watches too often,
hoping the frequency of checks will bring the bus sooner.
A jogger with her bottled water cedes to the incline,
the grandma with her brood hands each child
her own ticket.

The wheels serve them all, the long-haired and hairless,
the marrieds, the singles, the newly divorced,
double gendered and genderless, immigrants and natives.
All protagonists of their own stories. I back my car out of
    the garage,
pass them without acknowledging their starring roles in
    mine.

Honorable Mention, Alameda County Fair, 2017

Summary of Senses

I'm the scent of the white Asiatic lilies
at the burial site, the salt in the tears
of the widow, the sweat on the brow
of the gravedigger, the ache in the heart
of the family.

I'm the strain in the arm of the pallbearer,
the worry etched in the forehead lines
of the siblings, and the smell of exhaust
as cars leave the cemetery.

I am the soft landing of the golden disk
whose yellow, orange and red rays spread
to blanket the hallowed grounds
with warmth, peace, and grace.

I am the sound of the rusty hinge
on the gate swinging shut,
locking in the memory of the last farewell.

I am the summary of senses in sorrow
present when words can't suffice,
hidden in moments of grief
evidenced by inaudible sobs and silent embraces.

Published in *Quintessence*, Soul Poet Society, June 2021

Accepted for publication in *Balm 2*, Ravens Quoth Press

Fading

In my watercolor days
permanence loses its grip –
steely blue brushstrokes
loosen and slide into the sea.
Streaks of pigment break free,
start to bleed, form a new horizon.
Colors thin, dilute solid memories
and create a translucent wash that
bathes me in surrender
leaves me with a ghost painting.

Silver Ribbon Award, Alameda County Fair, 2016

Beat

A Beat generation poet,
once a beacon of The Word,
held forth last night in a
nearby library in the People's
Republic of Berkeley.
His reading anticipated,
the audience hushed,
his saxophonist brilliant,
yet I failed to connect.
The jazz and spoken word
fiercely clashed,
each fighting for the spotlight,
out of step, and,
more distraction still,
the event had not evolved
from the faded sixties.
As a relic it was true,
but resurrected it was old and tired.

I expected this handsome
gentleman with a shock
of white hair to trade in rubies,
diamonds, other gems,
but all we got were glass baubles.
He was stuck in a finger-snapping
self-adoration in an
out-of-sync era,
his orgasmic utterings
belonging in a bedroom
not a literary performance.
I offered him all:
pity, disappointment,
polite applause.

First Place and Best of Class, Flashback to the 60s: Poetry,
Marin County Fair, July 2017

TRUTH OR DARE

I wanted the truth to be beautiful and noble,
draped in white and carrying a torch.
Instead I found her naked, bald, and barefoot,
pouring out of the tap under no pressure,
unfiltered, raw , unrefined.
I expected a drumroll to announce her entrance
through velvet curtains,
yet found her an undistinguished guest
in the third row.
I pictured her aligned with huddled masses,
suckling babes at her breast,
but found her among the privileged
who were better able to afford her.
I imagined her showing up in court
with strong evidence,
but found she dwells in confessionals
and dance halls where she steps on toes,
and on reality shows with selected bites.
She is outed, but cannot be
warmed over or denied.
I dreamt of her fueling the nation,
roaring with conviction,
stoking the smoking engines
of logic and sanity.

Yet she sits cross-legged with ears plugged
by too much pleading,
eyes shut from too much color,
speechless to respond to what's self-evident.
She is unhurried and inconvenient.
Her first name is not gospel.
She's not what she should be,
but what is.
Accept her or not,
she will still be.
Amen.

Published in *The Wild Word*, July 2021

DROPLET

Unlike a tear
filled with fear
or joy
or sadness,
a raindrop jiggles its way
down the café window
on a leaky day.
Emotionless, it logically chooses
its path of descent,
veers left, halts, rethinks,
moves right, then intentionally
and purposefully
heads south with haste
as though late for a rendezvous.

Published in *Open Skies Quarterly,* Volume Five,
Anniversary Edition, 2021

Kintsukuroi

I am the shattered pottery,
my flaws no longer hidden
for I highlight them today.
I swallow the glowing lava,
feel it seep into the cracks
of my heart, the gaps
in my memory, the fractures
in my bones,
the mismatched alignment
of my skeletal chassis;
it fills the voids
with shimmering roadways
outlined in amber veins.
Its rivulets ooze
through internal crevasses,
create repair,
mend me
to showcase the stunning,
repurposed entity I've become
after being broken.

Leaves on a Stone Fence

Pebbles tumble from the wall
Jagged edges protrude
Missing chips leave hollows in the fence
Erosion has feasted on the stones
Yet spring returns with a loud green vine
as it girds the fence and gives it a spine.
It laps up the gray and imbues it with an aura
of jade and aroma of innocence, weaving
in and out of the joints to lace the cells together
to form a bond that will not separate
stone from life.

Silver Ribbon Award, Alameda County Fair, 2016

Pride Without the Fall

My parents loved me with accents
as thick as slow-moving syrup;
their tongues were not designed
for English vowels, nor had they
the accompanying gestures.
I always worried they wouldn't
be well understood and shielded
them with my protective apron
of translation covering up
their stained speech.

But the day came when I left
and pushed the fledglings out the nest,
to fly and land on their own.

They flew, although not in a straight line.
They zigged and zagged and landed
with a plop. Up they got up again and again
and again and kept lifting off.
What every child wants for her parents.

Published in *Life and Legends,* 10th edition, June 15, 2021

Bless Me

I am the sound of the cricket chirping a welcome
to the night of stars,

the crowing of the rooster awakening you to rise
to the music of the traffic.

I am the scales you practiced as a child
which made your teacher wince,

the dripping of the faucet grabbing your attention
when you don't want to hear.

I am the clicking of a pen by an absent-minded student
next to you in the library,

the winter raindrops on the tin roof tapping out a steady
    sequence
rhythmically challenged.

And all along you thought I was an inconvenient noise
and put up with my presence.

I am sound without judgment, the identifier of tones.
No tree falls without my accompaniment.

Without me you would miss the aria that casts a spell
    on you,
steals away your breath,

miss the lullaby that rocks you to sleep
and infuses your dreams.

Without me you would be monolingual and never speak
    in worldly tongues.
Bless me for reaching out to you.

Published by *The Wild Word* in its Winter Song issue, 2021

Spare Me

Don't push me off the canvas,
don't paint me out of the picture,
leave a corner for me, a bit of color,
a shadow, a glimmer of hope and life,
and I'll be forever grateful,
even for the negative space.

Accepted for publication in *Balm 2,* Ravens Quoth Press

A City in the Stans of Central Asia

From a distant land
the pull of ancient silk threads
tugs gently at my senses
rousing me from years of indifference,
daring me to come learn
from my place of birth
who I am not.
Borders do not nationalize me,
I cannot outrun distance.
Tashkent was but a midwife
birthing me in exile to refugees.
Yet, a draw to return,
own it or reject it,
taste the *plov* as its cuisine
and the independence it now has
from a jailer who held the Soviet keys.
What offense had it committed
against me? Why do I feel betrayed?
Perhaps our brief stay there
was endured knowing we would
be swept out like yesterday's trash
to wash upon another shore.
I prepare an Uzbeki valise
packed with low expectations
for my journey to a place
that never wanted me.

Published in *Slant: A Journal of Poetry*, 2017 edition

EVIDENCE OF THE WIND

Leaves rustle, hanging laundry dances
in rhythmic flaps
a wheat field parts a line in your hair
a flag wraps itself around a pole,
a patriotic Cuban cigar.

Its exhale keeps the kite aloft
Blows back the feathers of a headstrong bird
Whistles up a storm
Rocks the rolling foam-topped waves

Coaxes the hat off a hiker's head
Flings it across the hill
Chases away the cloud figures
I've conjured in my head
Fuels tornadoes in the flatlands
Travels with heat in desert landscapes

Taken to court and sued
You cannot prove it was involved

Published in *Quintessence*, Soul Poet Society, June 2021

CHARCOAL AND CHALK

One beckons me outdoors
Invites me to sketch with abandon
No fear, no restraint
Only free-range, light-spirited
Immersion in a medium of dry art

The other more serious
Engages me with rigor
Showcases shadings and negative space
Demands I earn each
Full-bodied black stroke

One invites the rainbow
Pastel-inspired
Carries forward from childhood
Temporary fun in the sun
On sidewalks and boardwalks

The other runs a short gamut
From black to gray
And few hues in between
A mere minor scale
The more colors I forgo
The deeper the quality
Tone and subtlety I uncover

Now mature, I've lost the colors
From my early years
I settle into darkness
Each shade a nuance.

Economy of Words

From her tiny coin purse
of compliments
she would frugally
distribute one now and then,
not at random,
but only when earned
with measured effort and heart.

The clasp would shut
to store the rest
till a glowing lyrical line
invited them out.

Over and over I tried
to earn one.
Over and over I failed,
until one day
the clasp opened for me
and I knew I would
try harder than ever
for another.

Published in *Open Skies Quarterly*, Volume Five,
Anniversary Edition, 2021

F is for Fiction

In the fifth season
the fall of light
produces false colors,
a fatal grace
fools me twice,
leaves me forever plucked.

I'm fortune's pawn at the
opposite end of happy,
falling to ash far from
the tree of life.

I slide down the shaft
like silver on glass,
follow the faces of strangers
to where I become
a feast for crows,
watching my funeral in beige.

Accepted for publication in *Balm 2*, Ravens Quoth Press

The Other Parent

You are the parent I don't write about,
the one who loved me in her own barricaded way
but couldn't say it aloud.
You overfed me; that was love.
I ate so kids in Russia wouldn't starve.
What you couldn't teach me I learned at school.
You taught me to distrust, be fearful, hide.
Yet you loved me in your own hunkered-down way.
You were not to blame for who you became.
The War and its aftermath did that to you, your sisters.
Each of you went mad, but you were the first.
I never wanted to be like you, to be so
dependent on a man, have no career.
I never wanted to look like you, but I failed.
I loved you in my own hesitating way too,
but like you, couldn't utter the words.
Car rides, oh the car rides
to and from the doctor's where
you did nothing but complain and express
your desire to die, droning on endlessly
in the midst of the depression
that was yours for so many years.
Yet you loved me in your own twisted way.

Even the radio turned up loud couldn't
mask your monotonous diatribe
I pretended not to hear – every sigh
and moan, a chink in my armor of hope.
And yet I went on to care for you
like daughters do, like no one else could or would.
In lucid times, you thanked me.
The other times you took me for granted,
yet you loved me in your own obstructive way.
Your ills, pains are now mine. I bond with you in disease.
Yet I loved you in my own disallowing way.
I swallowed the bitter medicine I was dosed;
it saddened and strengthened me, but I believe
you somehow knew I would be okay.

Trespassers All

By their very nature
they set limits, control entry,
monitor exits, exact tolls,
direct movement, create refugees,
force immigration.
These are what borders
and boundaries do.

Yet they leak and breach
as nature ignores their laws.
Coyotes and vultures pay no heed,
tumbleweeds roll across with abandon,
weeds follow as invaders,
streams flow across closed frontiers,
sand dunes sneak over the line,
mists hover over political divides.
Fog wraps us all,
citizens, critters, conifers
in a common blanket
of blind reliance.

But still, we, the humans for whom
borders were created, are born
into noncompliance
when we emerge –
trespassers into life. Sometimes
you must trespass to live.

Gladiolas in a White Vase

How do they prance while standing still?
They parade rooted in a vase
as they pose in the light's prism
and smile a rainbow's colors.
They need not yell nor jump
to sing out meaning.
Silence of awe is louder
than declarations of beauty
and longer remembered.
I live in their moment,
meditate on what they emit
grace, style, spirit.
I take their serenity
for my calm,
return to it when
I stumble on doubt.
Gladiolas in a white vase –
my icons of strength, innocence,
and pride.

Best of Show, San Mateo Country Fair, 2015

Bursting with Pride

The drumroll starts,
lights lower,
the star of the show
basks in anticipated admiration
awaiting her cue to shine –
with laser precision
the spotlight rays slice
through the velvet gray to
showcase her as the jewel she is,
multicolored, filtered by evening's lens,
and the sensuous umber of dusk.
A skyline of highlights, a precursor
to a scene engulfed in rain and darkness.
As she takes a bow
claps of thunder show their appreciation,
the curtains close,
torrents of drops fall
with no pity for the city of Guanajuato.

CURTAINS

My parents were from an empire
of lies, and I remain one of them,
a little white one.
From an iron curtain rusted
with ideals suspended over
foundations of clay and mud,
they tailored me to fit
a new western geographic.
I received a new name, a new age.
My voyage of discovery
built on villages of cards.

Always an immigrant,
the stigmas packed
in broken luggage, gray
angst of an elsewhere person,
waiting to be outed
like the wizard behind the curtain,
hoping to find safe haven
in my own little plot
of Kansas to savor whom
I have become and let go
of the stained receiving
blanket in which I was
wrapped at birth.

Best of Show Award, Alameda County Fair, 2016

Honorable Mention, Reuben Poetry Competition, Voices of Israel, 2017

Left Hanging in a Web

Once a majestic presence,
now a ruin among the weeds.
The sky pours its sunlight
into this box of fallen stones.
Graceful Moorish arches
still think they stand and serve,
but only as a reminder
of what once used to be.

Spotted off the main path,
it beckons me to come.
I find my way in past
the red-diagonal no-entry sign
to stand where I belong.
Two-story edifice
now one hundred eighty years gone,
emanating architectural influence
of Ottoman times
and holiness of spirit.

The circles of former domes
are windows for the faithful
resting on colorless pillars
sliding down from the women's
story to the men's.
The recessed ark
once cradled its Torah,
now absent as congregants.

Once a stained-glass window,
now a skeletal Mogen David
hanging in a web spun over decades,
transparent, unadorned, alone.
Once a regal temple,
a jewel near Bulgaria's Vidin,
today a relic known to few.
Hymns of congregants long gone or buried
still echo against the eastern wall.

As reddish gold wall of stones
glistens unfocused in dusk,
the stillness in the sanctuary
broken by the S'hma, Kol Nidre
and the prayer for the dead,
heard only in my head.

Having inhaled,
I turn to walk away,
take one more look back,
and say
Amen.

2020 Hindsight

In my kitchen I make soup,
chicken soup, of course, though
there's no schmaltz in the pantry.
Sorrow boils away in the stockpot,
only a trace of angst left behind
when I add the bird,
weep over a cut onion,
fill the house with silent scents,
swallow the elixir.

During this peculiar pause
we take a step back
to honor old school ways,
to bake with yeast, spring clean till July,
bring out the Singer, stitch in time,
and garden with ardor.

Yet also new steps to learn,
to dance with our deadly partner,
rechoreograph the movement,
let fear pass through.

Wait for a day without death
while I stock up on
servings of compassion
and discover it's
the eighth wonder.

Published in the *San Francisco Chronicle*, May 8, 2020

Published by Inspiration for Writers in *In the Midst: A Covid-19 Anthology*, November 2020

Mendocino Farms Sandwich Market

A young, olive-toned dark-haired hostess
rings up our order here in Burlingame
with a warm smile.
She belongs on the cover of Vogue.
Her perfectly white teeth dazzle us;
we can't help but stare.
So much beauty arresting us at lunch,
so much kindness, real or affected.
I notice her tanned forearm – a tattoo
in stylized Arabic.
May I ask what it says?
She reads it aloud, and I repeat it
as she patiently corrects me.
And its meaning?
I am at peace with myself.
And so she was.
Amira on her nametag.

Feminine of Amir, I ask.
She nods and smiles.
I am Palestinian, she shares.
I smile and walk away,
wondering if she saw my
Hebrew necklace. I turn back
and say *shukraan*. She smiles
and says, *very good*.
She and I so far from home,
polite and civil in our exchange,
wondering what the other thinks.
I smile and walk away, fearing
we could never be close friends,
but neither do we have to be
enemies.

Vellichor

Is it you I have to credit
for the subtle aroma
old paper pages emit
to entice me into stores
of secondhand books,
ancient tomes in libraries,
yellowed volumes
in stacks at universities?
I believe it is you, *lignin*.

Are you what keeps me
lingering in the aisles
inhaling the vanillin
you infused in paper?
It must be you.

To abandon your aroma
for cold, odorless screens
and recorded voices is to rip pages
from your soul and desert you
on an island with no rescue.
Olfactory satisfaction dies.

Lignin, your smell provides
what others wish they could:
a direct pathway to memory,
a conduit, a shortcut home.
You create in me a hunger
for knowledge, exploration,
which hardware cannot provide.

No Rhyme nor Reason

It's winter by the time
I cross the street.
No amount of coaxing
brings back even one day of fall.
The year flips through seasons
at the speed
of shuffled cards in a deck,
deals them in the wrong order.

Buds with no plans to bloom
do so without warning,
yellow jackets suit up to visit
more hospitable stamens,
the sky's traffic lanes
carry fowl with no passports.
I stand perpendicular on the corner
waiting for the signal to cross.

Golden Ribbon Award, Alameda County Fair, 2014

My Tsunami

You crumbled before me
like a pillar in an earthquake.
You liquefied like an iceberg
in a tsunami.
You were the strongest man
I knew, in morals and justice,
yet when your brother,
the last of your family,
died, your grief could not
contain itself. You burst
like a damn trying to hold
back floodwaters, and I
witnessed the sharpest
pain of all in your heart.

The wetness from your eyes
told me more than I could bear.
You shattered like a wine glass
falling on a ceramic tiled floor
creating shards that could never
be put back together again.
I had never seen you cry before,
never saw you cry again.
You, the last bridge from the old world
to this one, saw a weak dynasty
disappearing, and I, your daughter,
will never forget what it cost you.

I knew not how to bring you solace,
could only lay a bouquet of words at your feet
and hoped it would suffice.

3rd Place Award, San Mateo County Fair, 2018

Sounds of August

Summer exhales in tiny hisses –
Aspens let out sacred sighs that escape
through transparent clouds.
      I listen and salute them.
Amber and ocher drip
from auburn leaves to stain
the earth in matching colors.

Retiring leaves drop to pave
the footpaths with pop and crunch.
Chirps signal a return to home
in fledgling and empty nests.
Iridescent wings flutter as Monarchs cease
their rule and migrate in swarms.
      I accept the farewell.

A crisper breeze sweeps through
the brittle boughs
as the season tiptoes
away on bare feet.
      I bend with the boughs – to do
      otherwise would upset season and reason.
Autumn
is on the horizon.

Honorable Mention, San Mateo Country Fair, 2014

A Tablespoon of Salt

The gravesite service for my father,
The breakup delivered by phone,
The rejection from the publisher,
The essay my professor panned,
The soufflés that fell,
The hair perms that frizzed,
The yeast that never rose,
The scar that marked my tumor,
The cast that cradled my break,
The crash that totaled my car,
The birthday party few attended,
The diet that added pounds,
The prom I didn't go to,
The Valentine card I didn't get.

Life's recipe lacking salt
Will also lack joy.
Wash away the sorrows
And you wash away
The footprints of our lives.

Accepted for publication *in Balm 2, Psythur,* Ravens Quoth Press

Postcards and Bananas

On a wobbly three-legged stool
she balances her barrel-shaped body
white kerchief on brown hair
framing mud pie eyes
and rustic cheeks.
She bellows out from the side
of her stall on Lyab-i-Khauz in old Bukhara
the only two English words she knows:
Postcards, bananas.

Her booming voice spreads her message,
spanning the walkway, grabbing the attention
of tourists and strollers.
They turn to face her.
She smiles, exposing gaps in teeth
as her forearm leads your
eyes to her wares: scarfs, tote bags,
embroidered pouches, coats.

I see no postcards, see no bananas.
Disillusioned, I walk on accompanied
by the refrain of *Postcards and Bananas*
playing in my head.

First Place and Best of Class, San Mateo County Fair, 2020

Summer at a Price

Sun warms my sad pale cheeks,
Invites them to brief outdoor interludes,
To regain color and ruddiness,
Bleaches blond my top strands of hair,
Assures me it's here to stay, to linger
With me on a fried chicken picnic,
A salad lunch on a café patio,
A stroll around a swan-filled lake.

I want to believe, to hibernate no more.
I rely on it to bring me cheer,
Dissolve any thoughts of wintered gloom,
Fill my glasses to their rims,
Restore agility to my arthritic limbs,
Bathe me in resilience,
Restore my will to thrive.

High hopes I pin on an orb of shooting gas,
To deliver my favorite season,
My preferred quarter-slice of the year.
Foreplay is the spring, enticing me
To imagine the gifts summer will come bearing.
And then I am reminded that the warm, relaxed
Attitude of summer loses its perfume without the cold
Crispness of winter to mitigate its sweetness
And shape its temperament.

HALF THE HURRICANES

Born a female, I was handed
a manual of low expectations,
and warned to adhere to them.
A bullseye of shame on my back
marked me a target for arrows:
insults, regrets, obedience, demands.

Half the hurricanes bear our names,
a step up from having them all blamed on us,
but that is where equality ends.

Resentment planted a seed in me.
It fed on bitter nourishment
and thoughts of wrongs replayed,
justice a victim of inequity,
vengeance its mate.

Laments sent to heaven's door
evaporated on the way.
We're overdue for new
Thou Shalts and Shalt Nots.

Stale advice of "give it time,"
"it's God's way," and "look how far
you've come" deserves to
shrivel up like a slug in salt.

Heed my words. They crescendo
from a whistle to a roar,
turn deafening when unheeded.
Take them not in vain.
They are my legacy.

Stop battering me with your
self-righteous confidence
of knowing what's best for me.
I invite you to stand by my side
and call me friend, sister, peer, equal,
names you'd want the women
in your family called.

I'm still waiting and
will come round again whether
the world is ready or not,
like the hurricanes which bear our names.

Lessons from an Uneducated Master

An immigrant with broken English
stitching his way to tailoring mastery
cutting on and out bias
to pattern a life in America.

Education not bookish, diploma
not earned, certificate not awarded,
but smarts you couldn't define or deny
so that others held him in reverential awe.

With an algebraic work problem
I'd run to him, translate the poser,
answer in a second, but not the how.
That's your job, he said. *Now
you can start with the end in mind.*

Free 5th grade violin lessons
I feared to take.
No need to fear he reassured.
*Always try; you're not signing
up for life.* I heeded and later
joined the orchestra, played
through the end of high school.

Dad, can you teach me how to drive?
I asked at fourteen, too young for a permit.
In his '51 Chevy with a gray repair patch
he ignited my love for cars and driving.
Going down the street too slowly,
others honking at my crawl,
he'd say, *Just ignore the honking,*
Focus on your control.

Published in *My Father Taught Me*, Spirited Muse Press, 2021

Fading From View

Golden hills turn a rich tan,
poison oak slips out of it greasy green,
dresses up in red, masquerades
as royalty on carpets.
Aspens sparkle with hints of autumn,
and teen lovers part till next year.

Fairs have closed, cotton candy
and corn dogs deleted
from determined vendors.
Prizes packed away in storage trailers.
Ferris wheels no longer turn,
but leaves do, from green to rust.

Backpacks line the walls of ivy,
tether balls are slapped 'round poles,
We're in the season before discontent,
Labor Day is one of rest.
No more stalling, no denying,
evidence is clear, showing
summer is fading from view
and I shall have to adjust.

When Notes Become a Melody

The forest is more than a collection of trees
The sky is more than a meeting of clouds
Chili is more than a pot of beans
A village is more than a group of homes
A school is more than classes of students
A closet is more than some hanging clothes
A scalp holds more than a head of hair
A novel is more than a count of pages
A house is more than a series of rooms
All this becomes evident when
You understand how notes become a tune
Verses become a poem
And life becomes a choice

Arrival

When I shut my eyes
I am back on the freighter
making its way over the Atlantic
to a new home, new country,
a foreign place.

Too young to know
what I'll miss in the old country,
too alien to be accepted in the new,
too language-limited to converse,
and too naïve to care.

When I open my eyes
the present shakes me awake,
slaps me into consciousness,
shoves me out the door
to grapple with the now.

Too old to make new waves,
too fearful of our future,
too passionate about freedom,
wise enough to see the land I'm in
becoming the lands I left.

When I shut my eyes again
I'm still on my voyage;
I haven't yet
reached the shore.

Published in *Litehouse*, 2021

Silver Medal, Alameda County Fair, 2019

Acknowledgments

I am deeply grateful to all East Bay poets in groups I have met with in person and on Zoom who have offered me support, suggestions, and valuable feedback on my work. Thank you, Tuesday Night Poets, Thursday Night Poets, Pinole Library Writing Group, Prescient Poets, and POV poets.

My heartfelt appreciation goes to Hilary Roberts, my patient editor, who guided me gently and intentionally to make hard decisions and redo poems I didn't think I could improve any more. She was right.

To my deep listener, Margaret (Peggy) Lucke, a writer, teacher, and publisher of merit whose advice made so much sense once I heard it from her. I was so fortunate to have her ear as she prepared to publish my book. I always looked forward to our sessions outdoors at the Pinole Starbucks where I could feel progress as I sipped my mocha.

To my husband Carl I owe gratitude for having faith in me, expressing it, and spending unaccompanied binge time in front of the TV while I met in so many Zoom groups he lost count of them.

I thank all my friends and readers of my poems along the way and those who listened to me present. Your interest in my work motivated me and inspired me to gather the pieces into a whole based on your advice.

About the Author

*E*vie Groch enjoys writing poetry, along with short stories, memoirs, travelogues, opinion pieces, and letters to the editor. An educator as well as a writer, she seeks teachable moments in her work in which to inject universal messages, pose challenging questions, test ethics, and inspire readers with a joy of language.

The themes of travel, language, immigration, and justice are special for her, and she peppers her writing with words from a variety of world languages, several of which she speaks. She cannot live without humor and has learned to hone hers in presentations and writing. She also likes recipes, cooking, word challenges, and puzzles she completes or creates for others.

She lives and writes in Northern California. She graduated from UCLA and earned postgraduate degrees from UC Berkeley and California State University. Currently she is working in the area of supervision for teachers going into administration and those newly credentialed for administration.

Her writing has won her recognition and awards. She is the author of *What Do You Bring to the Table?*, a book about food, family and friends. Her work has been published by Women's Federation for World Peace in Canada and Grand Circle Travel, and has also appeared in *The New York Times*, the *San Francisco Chronicle*, the *Contra Costa Times*, *THE Journal; Games* magazine and many online venues.

Some magazines, journals, and reviews that carry her poems are *The Wild Word Magazine; Whimsical Poet: A Journal of Contemporary Poetry; Necroproductions; The*

Pangolin Review; Sage Soup Literary Magazine; Open Door Poetry Magazine; Dyst Literary Journal; Slant: A Journal of Poetry; and *Borders and Boundaries: Poems by Finalists.*

Her poems and short stories can also be found in such anthologies as *Balm 2,* published by Ravens Quoth Press; *Between the Fault Lines,* published by Sugartown Publishing; *Carry the Light Anthology,* published by Sand Hill Review Press; *My Father Taught Me,* published by Spirited Muse Press; *My Robot & Me,* published by The Red Penguin; *Quintessence: Aspects of the Soul,* published by the Soul Poetry Society; and *Touching: Poems of Love,* published by *Open Door* Magazine.

www.ingramcontent.com/pod-product-compliance
Lightning Source LLC
LaVergne TN
LVHW051842080426
835512LV00018B/3030